BIRMINGHAM 1963

HOW A PHOTOGRAPH RALLIED CIVIL RIGHTS SUPPORT

by Shelley Tougas

Content Adviser: Steve Remy, PhD, Associate Professor of History, Brooklyn College, City University of New York

Reading Adviser: Alexa L. Sandmann, EdD, Professor of Literacy, College and Graduate School of Health, Education, and Human Services, Kent State University

COMPASS POINT BOOKS

a capstone imprint

Compass Point Books
1710 Roe Crest Drive
North Mankato, MN 56003

Editor: Jennifer Fretland VanVoorst
Designer: Tracy Davies
Media Researcher: Wanda Winch
Library Consultant: Kathleen Baxter
Production Specialist: Sarah Bennett

Image Credits
Alamy: Black Star/Charles Moore, 8, 9, 18, 24, 39, 40, 53; AP Images, 37, 49, 50-51,
Bill Hudson, 30, Horace Cort, 26; Black Star: Charles Moore, Cover, 11, 32, 55; Corbis:
Bettmann, 6, 29; Getty Images: Buyenlarge, 46, *New York Daily News* Archive, 43, *New
York Daily News* Archive/John Duprey, 5, 35, Popperfoto/Rolls Press, 45, SSPL/*Daily
Herald* Archive, 23, Time Life Pictures/Burton Mcneely, 16, 52; Library of Congress,
Prints and Photograph Division, 13, 15; Tim Mantoani Photography, 19; Wisconsin
Historical Society/Hunter Gray (John R. Salters) Papers/Fred Blackwell, 21.

Library of Congress Cataloging-in-Publication Data
Tougas, Shelley.
  Birmingham 1963: how a photograph rallied civil rights support / by Shelley
Tougas.
      p. cm. — (Compass point books. Captured history.)
  Includes bibliographical references and index.
    ISBN 978-0-7565-4398-3 (library binding)
    ISBN 978-0-7565-4446-1 (paperback)
 1. Civil rights movements—Alabama—Birmingham—History—20th century—
Juvenile literature. 2. African American children—Alabama—Birmingham—
History—20th century—Juvenile literature. 3. African Americans—Civil rights—
Alabama—Birmingham—History—20th century—Juvenile literature.
4. Birmingham (Ala.)—Race relations—History—20th century—Juvenile literature.
5. Moore, Charles, 1931–2010—Influence—Juvenile literature. I. Title.
  F334.B69T68 2011
   323.1196'0730761781—dc22   2010038574

Visit Compass Point Books on the Internet at *www.capstonepub.com*

Printed in the United States of America in North Mankato, Minnesota.
042016   009726R

TABLEOFCONTENTS

Chapter One

THE CHILDREN MARCH

The students knew they would be arrested. Yet they swarmed to the 16th Street Baptist Church, the headquarters of the civil rights movement in Birmingham, Alabama. Boys and girls. Football players, cheerleaders, and student council members. Teenagers and children as young as 8. Young African-Americans who wanted the same rights as white citizens.

On May 3, 1963, 14-year-old Carolyn Maull skipped school to meet at the church and march with hundreds of other students. After hearing civil rights leaders speak at her church, Carolyn wanted to be part of an important movement to end racial discrimination. Local civil rights leaders had organized a march to demand an end to segregation in restaurants, shops, hotels, and other businesses. They called the protest the Children's Crusade.

Temperatures approached 80 degrees Fahrenheit (27 degrees Celsius) that day, but there was too much noise for Carolyn to enjoy the spring day as she marched along. She couldn't even hear birds chirping in nearby Kelly Ingram Park. Students were singing freedom songs as they marched. Police dogs barked and growled. From the sidewalks, African-American adults shouted at police.

Carolyn knew police planned to round up the young demonstrators and take them to jail. The day before, police had arrested hundreds of young people for trying to march

Young protesters marched in the streets of Birmingham, Alabama, as part of the Children's Crusade.

into the white shopping district. The children had wanted to talk to the city's mayor about desegregating downtown stores. Carolyn also knew police might turn attack dogs loose on the crowd. The people who organized the demonstration had warned kids about the police and the dogs.

But nobody had told Carolyn about firefighters with hoses. Near the park firefighters stood like warriors. They pointed their hoses at the marchers, ready to force back students with blasts of water. When a fire hose is turned on half strength, the water can knock a person to the ground. At full strength, it can strip bark off a tree and tear a brick from a building.

Birmingham's commissioner of public safety, Eugene "Bull" Connor, was determined to stop the students immediately. If the young people managed to reach downtown Birmingham, the firefighters would lose the chance to turn the hoses on them. They couldn't take a

Young African-Americans gathered in the streets to rally in support of their civil rights.

chance that the water would hit white shoppers and white businesspeople.

Carolyn paused to see what would happen next. At that moment, the fire hoses sprayed the crowd at half strength. Some of the students sat down on the sidewalk and refused to move. They didn't try to fight back. Organizers had taught them how to protest without using violence.

Police and firefighters responded with more force. The hoses blasted at full strength. One by one, students who had been standing toppled to the ground. Those who were sitting were swept down the street like twigs in a raging river. Carolyn, however, stood near a building. When the water hit her small body, it smashed her and two others against the wall.

"The water stung like a whip and hit like a cannon," said Carolyn, whose married name is McKinstry. "The force of it knocked you down like you weighed only 20 pounds, pushing people around like rag dolls. We tried to hold onto the building, but that was no use."

Connor ordered police to release the dogs, which snarled and bit demonstrators. Adult onlookers were angry. They threw bottles, stones, and bricks at police. News reporters snaked through the demonstration, trying to record the event without getting hurt. The police barricade caused traffic snarls throughout downtown. A white driver tried to run his car into a line of African-American students.

Downtown Birmingham was erupting. Police, firefighters, and protest leaders agreed that the situation was becoming

"We tried
to hold onto
the building,
but that was
no use."

EUGENE "BULL" CONNOR

The name Eugene "Bull" Connor became a synonym for racial intolerance in American history.

Civil rights leaders needed the news media to win their fight against segregation in Birmingham. To get the journalists interested, though, leaders needed conflict and drama. Commissioner of Public Safety Eugene "Bull" Connor gave them both. Connor firmly believed in segregation, but he unintentionally helped the civil rights leaders win their battle. When African-Americans—many of them children—marched in Birmingham, Connor ordered a brutal response. Police turned dogs loose on the crowd. Firefighters blasted people with powerful hoses. News coverage turned Americans' attention to the confrontation, and their outrage built support for civil rights laws.

Connor was not known to be a member of the Ku Klux Klan, a group whose members believe black people belong to an inferior race. But Connor supported the KKK's racist goals and violent tactics. He also protected the KKK from police action when its members bombed homes and beat African-Americans. In 1961 he delayed a police response, which allowed Klansmen to attack people challenging segregation. Several of the protesters, who called themselves Freedom Riders, were seriously injured. As racial tension built throughout the South, Connor became the face of police brutality.

Birmingham's business community and voters eventually turned against Connor. He'd created too much negative publicity for the city. Connor died from a stroke in 1973. He remains a symbol of racial intolerance in American history.

Photographer Charles Moore captured police dogs attacking protesters in Birmingham.

much too dangerous. The leaders decided to stop the demonstration and send the children home.

When Carolyn returned to her house, she was wet and exhausted. The water had matted her hair and ripped her sweater. Her muscles ached, and bruises were beginning to form where the water had hit her. Carolyn's parents were outraged. They had not given her permission to skip school. They ordered her to stay out of trouble and keep away from the demonstrators. The family didn't need problems with the police.

Carolyn's afternoon of protesting ended with torn clothes and angry parents. It seemed as if the day's trouble had been for nothing. Despite the marchers' efforts, Birmingham's white businesspeople showed little interest in meeting the demands of protest organizers. The organizers worried that lawmakers and ordinary Americans would continue to ignore the suffering caused by segregation.

But Carolyn Maull was about to call the world's attention to what was happening. That day a 32-year-old news photographer named Charles Moore had snapped a picture of Carolyn and two teen boys being slammed against a building by a blast of water. When people across the country saw the photo, they were stunned by the harsh treatment.

"I didn't want the firemen to get mad," Moore said decades later. "I just wanted everyone to see how hard the water looked as it hit them in the back. It's not about me. It's the photographs, and the photograph meant something."

Americans could no longer deny or ignore the fact that the country was split into two worlds. There was a world of opportunity if your skin was white, but there was a world of closed doors if your skin was black. African-Americans who tried to push open those doors risked their lives.

Suddenly the civil rights movement was bigger than Birmingham, bigger than a handful of southern states. The image of a 14-year-old girl's brutal treatment made civil rights a national problem needing a national solution.

"It's not about me. It's the photographs, and the photograph meant something."

Charles Moore's photograph of three teenagers forced against a building by water from a fire hose helped rally support for the civil rights movement.

A century after slavery officially ended, and a year after Carolyn's photo stunned the nation, Congress finally passed laws to give equal rights to citizens regardless of color.

Chapter Two

THE GROWTH OF CONSCIENCE

Charles Moore grew up in Alabama in the better half of the two worlds. His family wasn't rich, but his skin was white. In northern Alabama—and much of the South—skin color determined where people ate, shopped, lived, and went to school. When Moore needed water from a drinking fountain, he went to the fountain marked with a "whites only" sign.

African-Americans hadn't gained real freedom even though Congress had approved the 13th Amendment in 1865. The constitutional amendment banned slavery in America, but state and local governments in the South passed laws to segregate the races. Known as "Jim Crow" laws, they drew a dividing line between white and black citizens. Black people were considered second-class citizens, and this second-class treatment reached into every part of daily life. It wasn't uncommon to see a grown African-American man call a young white boy "sir."

Although racial tension swirled around Moore, who was born in 1931, his home life was different. Moore's father was a minister who sometimes preached in African-American churches. He wouldn't allow people to use racial slurs in his family's home.

"My dad told me, 'Son, you don't treat people badly because they are a different color,'" Moore said.

The Moore family's views were not shared widely.

"My dad told me, 'Son, you don't treat people badly because they are a different color.'"

Jim Crow laws kept African-Americans separate from whites.

Regardless of color, most citizens in the South quietly accepted segregation as a way of life. African-Americans who challenged segregation faced severe consequences. Legally, they could be arrested and charged with a crime. And white residents might beat or even kill African-Americans for behavior they didn't like, such as insulting a white woman. Police often overlooked crimes against black people.

Violence was preached and practiced by a group known as the Ku Klux Klan. The all-white group, which also opposed the Catholic and Jewish religions, wanted black people to remain second-class citizens. Klansmen attacked African-Americans and bombed their homes with little fear of arrest. In Birmingham racial violence became so common that people began calling the city "Bombingham."

The modern American civil rights movement began in the mid-1950s. During that time the United States Supreme Court ruled that black children suffered from laws forcing them into separate schools. The court's decision meant that public schools had to begin mixing races.

The decision helped to spark the campaign for civil rights. African-American leaders finally had legal support to fight for equal rights under the law. So did average citizens. In 1955 Rosa Parks, a seamstress and the secretary for the Montgomery, Alabama, chapter of the National Association for the Advancement of Colored People (NAACP), refused to give up her bus seat to a white rider. She was arrested as a result. Her arrest energized and unified African-Americans in Montgomery. They started a bus boycott, which meant

Rosa Parks was arrested and fingerprinted after refusing to give up her bus seat to a white rider. The boycott prompted by her action helped energize the civil rights movement.

they refused to use public transportation until they could sit where they wanted. The boycott lasted a year and drained the bus system of fares.

Suddenly the conflict over civil rights was national news. Names of African-American civil rights leaders such as Martin Luther King Jr., Ralph Abernathy, and Fred Shuttlesworth began to capture headlines. Rosa Parks would become known as the "mother of the modern-day civil rights movement."

CIVIL RIGHTS LEADERS

Fred
Shuttlesworth

Ralph Abernathy

Martin Luther King Jr.

Ralph Abernathy, Martin Luther King Jr., and Fred Shuttlesworth gathered with other black leaders at a funeral in Birmingham.

Martin Luther King Jr. is the most famous civil rights leader in American history. A talented speaker and writer, he motivated thousands of Americans to join the fight for equal rights. In 1968, when he was just 39, he was shot and killed by James Earl Ray, a white man. But King was not a lone warrior in the fight for civil rights.

Fred Shuttlesworth helped King found the Southern Christian Leadership Conference, one of America's most important civil rights groups. As a pastor and civil rights leader, Shuttlesworth supported principles of nonviolent activism.

Members of the Ku Klux Klan beat Shuttlesworth and his wife when they tried to enroll their children in an all-white school. Doctors were amazed that he didn't receive a serious head injury. Shuttlesworth famously said, "Doctor, the Lord knew I lived in a hard town, so he gave me a hard head."

Ralph Abernathy, a co-founder of SCLC, became its leader after King was murdered in 1968. He completed King's plan to hold a Poor People's Campaign in Washington, D.C. Abernathy also helped organize the bus boycott in Montgomery and many other campaigns. In a speech King described Abernathy as the best friend that he had in this world. King died in Abernathy's arms after being shot in Memphis, Tennessee.

Like other civil rights leaders, Abernathy paid a heavy price for his work. Racists beat him, bombed his home, and threatened his family. He was arrested dozens of times during demonstrations. Abernathy died in 1990 at age 64.

Rosa Parks helped to spark a successful campaign against segregation in 1955. Police arrested her when she refused to give up her bus seat to a white passenger. She worked with activists on the Montgomery bus boycott.

The controversy caused Parks to lose her job at a department store. She later worked as a secretary for a congressman and gave speeches around the country. Parks died in 2005.

> **"To be honest, I was a young kid. I didn't know what was going on in the world."**

But Moore paid little attention to the news. He'd never heard of Rosa Parks. Moore studied photography in California after serving in the Marines. He wanted to be a nature or fashion photographer, a job that would let him take pictures of the world's beauty. Newspapers were not glamorous or full of beauty.

"To be honest, I was a young kid. I didn't know what was going on in the world. I had no interest. My head was into camping, wildlife and fashion," Moore said.

But Moore needed a job, and he returned to Alabama to look for work. After a short time working at a portrait studio, he took a job at the *Montgomery Advertiser*. "So I got a job, and it turned my life around. I mean it literally turned my life around," Moore said. "Because I had found something that's more important than fashion or commercials or whatever, or even more important than money."

The newspaper office was blocks away from a church with a passionate African-American preacher named Martin Luther King Jr. The civil rights movement was about to ignite, and King was one of the sparks. From the moment Moore heard one of King's sermons, he knew the young preacher could be an important leader. King's strong and powerful voice captivated listeners. He spoke with conviction about the need for equal rights, and people listened. Moore recalled, "I became fascinated [by the] power of his [sermons.] From then on I wanted to cover him. I wanted every assignment I could get."

One day in September 1958, police arrested King for

loitering near a government building. King was waiting for his fellow pastor and friend Ralph Abernathy, who was inside the building at a court hearing. Police roughed King up as they hauled him to jail. Moore happened to be the only photographer on the scene. His photograph of the young preacher's mistreatment as he was being booked into jail was published in *Life* magazine, at the time the country's most

Charles Moore was the only photographer to capture Martin Luther King Jr. being manhandled by police after being arrested for loitering.

Charles Moore was photographed holding one of his first important images—the *Life* photo of Martin Luther King Jr. being booked into jail.

influential media outlet. The photo caused national outrage. African-Americans weren't alone in their anger. Many white readers were stunned that police would act harshly during a nonviolent disagreement—a disagreement not involving a common criminal but a minister.

The photo was important for several reasons. It marked the beginning of Moore's career photographing the civil rights movement. But it also was a lesson to King about the media's impact. A powerful photo could make people angry. It could motivate them to act, to fight for change. People didn't need to read the news story to feel emotional about an event. Without any other information, a photo could stir up anger, conflict, pain, fear, and countless other feelings. Words weren't needed. This meant that civil rights leaders could use photographs to gain support for their cause.

In 1962 Moore left the newspaper to begin a freelance career. Soon Moore was traveling across the South making a visual record of the civil rights movement. Many of his photographs appeared in *Life*. He photographed the violent reaction when the first black student enrolled at the University of Mississippi. Moore and his camera followed the Freedom Riders, a group of people who traveled across the South testing the Supreme Court's ruling desegregating bus stations. When civil rights leaders confronted segregation in Selma, Alabama, Moore was there.

The civil rights movement slowly won support, including support from white citizens. Americans who hadn't paid attention to segregation in the South could no longer ignore it. When they opened newspapers and magazines or watched television, they were confronted with images of mistreatment and demonstrations. Moore and other journalists gave Americans a behind-the-scenes look at the ugly side of the South.

For King and other civil rights leaders, progress was neither fast nor smooth. Their early battles taught them several things. First, they needed to motivate African-Americans to join the movement. Second, they needed to win the sympathy of white citizens to support change. To do both, they needed reporters and photographers. And to attract reporters and photographers, they needed conflict and drama.

Civil rights protesters staged a lunch counter sit-in. Their commitment to nonviolence was often challenged.

That key lesson was driven home in Albany, Georgia. African-American leaders in Albany wanted to fight segregation in their city. One of them invited King to speak at a rally. King was so moved by the rally's response that he and his civil rights organization, the Southern Christian Leadership Conference (SCLC), agreed to help the movement in Albany. The successful bus boycott in Montgomery had energized them to try another campaign.

But the Albany movement hit a wall. Police Chief Laurie Pritchett was a smart man and a firm believer in segregation. Pritchett refused to let Albany turn into Montgomery. He studied the movement's strategy and used it to his advantage.

King and other civil rights leaders had adopted principles of nonviolence. Following leaders such as Indian activist Mahatma Gandhi, they planned to refuse to obey the segregation laws. However they disobeyed peacefully. They would not destroy property in demonstrations, nor would they hurt anyone who opposed them. If police—or white citizens—attacked African-American demonstrators, the demonstrators would kneel down and pray. When too many demonstrators were arrested to be held in the jails, the media paid attention. African-Americans grew angry and supported the campaigns with their time and money. Most important, public officials and ordinary white citizens were forced to face the effects of segregation.

Chief Pritchett had studied Gandhi and the Montgomery campaign. He watched how the media covered the civil rights movement and noticed how lawmakers, white citizens, and

MAHATMA GANDHI

"I object to violence because when it appears to do good, the good is only temporary; the evil it does is permanent."—Mahatma Gandhi

Mohandas K. Gandhi, known as Mahatma Gandhi, is considered the father of nonviolent activism. His leadership helped secure India's freedom from Britain in 1947. Although he wasn't the first to practice principles of nonviolence and civil disobedience, he gained fame for successfully spreading the tactic among large numbers of people.

Many Indians believed they needed weapons and violent revolt to win freedom. Gandhi had other ideas. Indians, he said, must refuse to cooperate with the corrupt government. He urged Indians to boycott British products, ignore British customs, and refuse to pay taxes.

Gandhi energized the masses. Although his family was well-placed in society, Gandhi preached and lived a simple life. His experience in organizing people began in South Africa, where he lived and worked as a young man. When he returned to India, he led movements against discrimination. He also fought to help the poor, resolve conflict between religious groups, and strengthen women's rights.

Martin Luther King Jr. adopted Gandhi's principles for the civil rights movement in the United States. King said, "Christ gave us the goals and Mahatma Gandhi the tactics."

Gandhi's refusal to follow certain laws led to his arrest, and he served time in both South African and Indian prisons. Gandhi was shot and killed in 1948 by a Hindu fanatic. Today Gandhi is called the father of India.

Mahatma *means "Great Soul" in Sanskrit, the classical language of India.*

African-Americans reacted to the news stories and photos. Pritchett decided to carefully prepare his department's response. He wouldn't allow the media to cast the police as the villains and the demonstrators as innocent victims.

So when the Albany campaign began in December 1961, police behaved calmly and respectfully in front of the cameras. When demonstrators knelt to pray, Pritchett took off his hat and bowed his head. When police arrested demonstrators, they used their best manners and treated them gently. Pritchett even assigned 24-hour protection for

Nonviolent protesters were trained to drop to their knees and pray when confronted.

King, who hadn't wanted the security. Pritchett wanted to make sure the Klan didn't hurt King while he was in Albany.

The campaign couldn't generate a victims-and-bullies media story. Even potential stories about jailed civil rights leaders were scaled back. Demonstrators had prepared to spend many days in jail, but white citizens who supported segregation arranged to pay their bail. Officials released the demonstrators and sent them home.

"I've been thrown out of a lot of places in my day," said Ralph Abernathy, a civil rights leader, "but never before have I been thrown out of a jail."

Peaceful demonstrations, peaceful arrests, and peaceful releases? National news reporters and photographers yawned. This was not news.

Meanwhile, organizers realized that the Albany campaign suffered from a lack of a detailed plan. They'd set a goal of challenging segregation generally, rather than focusing on specific instances of it. Because the goal was vague and large, it was difficult to claim even small victories. Local African-Americans weren't motivated. Leaders failed to persuade the black population to join the fight.

On the other hand, Montgomery's black community had been committed to the boycott in that city. Historians estimate that 90 percent of African-Americans there had boycotted public transportation following Rosa Parks' arrest. For a year thousands of African-Americans had walked to school and work. Their refusal to ride buses had put financial pressure on the bus system. But in Albany only 5 percent

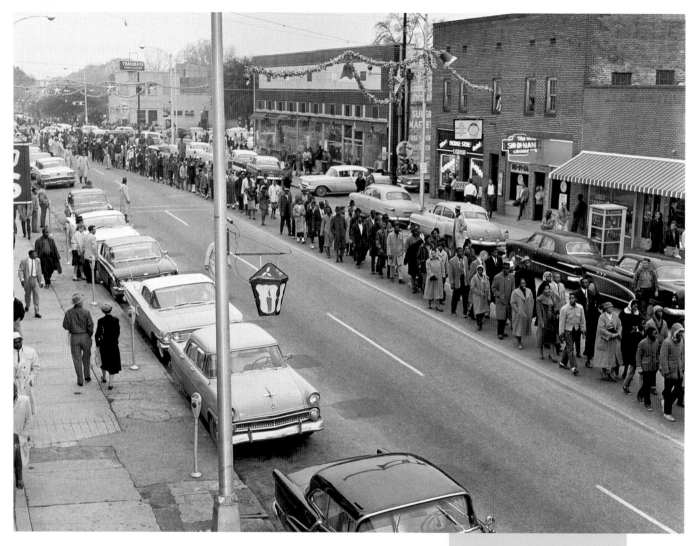

African-American protesters in Albany, Georgia, rallied in support of civil rights.

of African-Americans joined the effort. In fact, some of them ignored King's plea for nonviolence. They threw rocks and bottles at police. Their actions helped direct sympathy toward police instead of toward the demonstrators.

The Albany campaign collapsed. King and other civil rights leaders left the city under a cloud of failure.

When Fred Shuttlesworth, a co-founder of SCLC, asked King and others to launch a campaign in Birmingham, King worried about hurting the movement with another weak campaign. Civil rights leaders couldn't afford to repeat the Albany disaster, but Birmingham was an important target. Known as the most segregated city in the South, Birmingham seemed the perfect battleground for the war on segregation. King accepted the invitation.

This time leaders didn't rush. They worked out a plan for Birmingham with reasonable, defined goals. Leaders named the campaign Project C (for Confrontation), and they chose segregated businesses as their target. Determined to break the back of segregation, King went to Birmingham in 1963. Journalists, including Charles Moore, followed.

Project C launched with a whimper. Organizers struggled to find enough demonstrators willing to go to jail. Many of Birmingham's African-Americans distrusted the visiting civil rights leaders. What if they made the situation worse? What if they stirred up trouble for local black people and then abandoned them? What if employers fired demonstrators? What if the Klan bombed their homes?

Birmingham's white residents urged the African-American community to be patient. They dangled promises of change, like a letter to the editor in the *Birmingham Post-Herald* written by Thomas T. Coley of Ensley, Alabama. "Can't the local Negroes understand that all they have to do is wait a little longer?" Coley wrote. "Then certain white businessmen, politicians and clergymen with the help of our daily local newspapers, will hand them, on a silver platter, more than could ever be gained by marches, sit-ins and

"Can't the local Negroes understand that all they have to do is wait a little longer?"

kneel-ins. And there would be no need for going to jail or paying fines."

At that point, Birmingham's African-Americans were not going to jail. They steered clear of the demonstrations. Civil rights organizers realized that if they couldn't pack the jails, they'd lose the media's interest. If they lost the media's interest, they'd lose their connection to the American public.

The Reverend James Bevel, a young civil rights leader with SCLC, had a different idea. He believed that if organizers focused their work on recruiting demonstrators, the media would follow. "In a movement you don't deal with the press," he said. "You act like there is no press. Otherwise you end up staging it. A movement is when people actually do out of conviction."

Skilled in organizing groups, Bevel pushed a radical plan: The campaign should recruit children. Students didn't fear for their jobs. They dreamed of a different future, one in which they could eat, shop, and work where they wanted. Where parents saw risk, children saw hope.

Bevel recruited athletes and school leaders, who in turn recruited their classmates. DJs at black radio stations called for young people to get involved in the march. Thursday, May 2, was known as "D-Day"—the day when the students would skip school to protest segregation.

Bevel's strategy worked. Children provided the numbers the campaign needed. Over the next five days, kids demonstrated with toothbrushes in their pockets so they'd be ready for jail. Singing freedom songs, they marched out

"You act like there is no press. Otherwise you end up staging it. A movement is when people actually do out of conviction."

Young protesters in Birmingham practiced nonviolence and kept up their spirits by singing and dancing in the streets.

of the 16th Street Baptist Church into the white shopping district. When Commissioner of Public Safety Connor ordered the use of fire hoses and attack dogs despite the demonstrators' ages, the brutality of police and firefighters gave the campaign its villains. African-American adults were motivated to join the movement.

"They knew that they needed the right adversary," said Leslie Jack, a reporter who covered the movement. "And they picked the person—Bull Connor, the police commissioner—

Police led a group of children to jail following their arrest for protesting racial discrimination.

knowing that if they marched down into that Kelly Ingram Park that they would be confronted by dogs and fire hoses and violence. And the violence would get into the national media and therefore arouse the conscience of this country. And, of course, that's exactly what happened."

Over the next five days, thousands more people joined the children to march in the streets. They marched despite threats of jail, despite snarling dogs, despite powerful fire hoses. And Americans watched in horror.

ChapterThree
RALLYING THE NATION

Charles Moore had a reputation as the photographer most able to gain access to the front lines of the civil rights movement. This access served him well on May 3, 1963. The previous day's marches had been peaceful, but radio reports on the second day of the Children's Crusade suggested that things were about to turn violent. Bull Connor had instructed the police to use their attack dogs and firefighters to turn their hoses on the crowd.

As Carolyn Maull and the other children were marching toward downtown, Moore and reporter Michael Durham drove into Birmingham. Their paths crossed in a dramatic moment forever captured on film. Moore recalled, "We were driving into Birmingham to cover [the protest], and this is exactly what I saw. I said, 'Stop the car now,' and I got out and took that. I knew it was the shot." Over the next several days, Moore went on to take many more photos, but none has had more influence than the image of Carolyn Maull and two other teenagers slammed against a building by a blast of water.

Moore's photos of the Children's Crusade appeared in *Life* magazine May 17 with bold headlines: "The Spectacle of Racial Turbulence in Birmingham," "They Fight a Fire That Won't Go Out," "The Dogs' Attack Is Negroes' Reward," "The Hatreds Grow as Indignities Mount," and "Query for Southern Whites—What Now?" The photo of Carolyn Maull

"I said, 'Stop the car now,' and I got out and took that. I knew it was the shot."

The age of Moore's subjects—and the gender of Carolyn Maull—inspired protective feelings in the American public and helped rally support for the civil rights movement.

and two other young protesters took up an entire page.

The photos and article sparked an immediate response from the American public. The angry reaction would have been local instead of national if the photo had appeared only in the Birmingham newspaper. "Local Southern newspapers were not gung-ho to tell the story of the black struggle against the evils of the prevailing system," said William Raspberry, a columnist for *The Washington Post*. "The first response of the local papers in the South was to ignore the fledgling Movement, and the second was to blame it on outside agitators."

But in the 1960s, more than half of American adults regularly read *Life*. Not only was Carolyn's mistreatment displayed in the country's most influential publication, but *Life* dedicated 11 pages of photos and text to the Birmingham campaign.

Moore's photograph stunned Americans for several reasons. As unarmed teenagers, the protesters posed little threat to authorities. Yet they were attacked by firefighters, who for decades have been ranked among the most admired people in America. Firefighters risk their lives to save people. Americans were shocked to see their heroes hurting children. Dick Gregory, a popular African-American comedian, came to Birmingham to join the march partly because he was disturbed by the use of fire hoses. Firefighters had been his childhood heroes. He knew police confronted demonstrators because their job included crowd control, but firefighters' work was different.

In fact, Birmingham's firefighters were not accustomed to public confrontation. They put out fires, went to accidents, and took care of the city's fire equipment and fire stations. The firefighters' national union officially opposed using fire equipment as a way to control people. Not only was the tactic ethically controversial, but it also didn't work well. Hoses needed tankers or hydrants to blast water, and demonstrators could simply move their protest elsewhere.

Many of Birmingham's firefighters didn't want to be part of the response. They argued that the demonstration was a police matter, but city officials pressed them into service. Moore said that when the hoses sprayed the crowd, one firefighter told him, "We're supposed to fight fires, not people."

The firefighters' discomfort, however, didn't matter. Photos don't provide background information or offer insight into people's minds. The firefighters aren't even shown in the photograph. Moore's lens focused on the young people reeling from the blast of water. The photo froze a moment in time, a moment that left its viewers understanding the children's fear and pain—not what the firefighters were thinking.

But while the photo made viewers understand the experience of the protesters, it also suggested that the viewers themselves may have had some responsibility for the situation. The fact that the viewer does not see who was aiming the hose at the demonstrators implicates the whole nation in the attack. It suggests that by continuing to support, ignore, or deny racism and segregation, the entire country had

"We're supposed to fight fires, not people."

A group of protesters struggled to stay upright against the force of the fire hoses.

turned on the protesters. America itself held the hose.

The age of the photo's subjects also increased the public's sense of outrage. Adults instinctively want to protect children. Americans were deeply disturbed to see children victimized by the very people from whom they should expect protection.

What the photo couldn't convey was the controversy surrounding the use of young demonstrators. Even King had reservations about the Children's Crusade. If kids were hurt, King thought, Americans would be just as angry with the people who recruited them as with the people who attacked them. He and other leaders would be accused of putting children in danger.

Many African-Americans voiced strong opposition when organizers began recruiting students. The plan almost broke the partnership among civil rights leaders. Black teachers ordered their students to ignore the demonstration and stay in class. The principal of Birmingham's Parker High School even locked the front gates to prevent students from leaving.

Malcolm X, a prominent African-American activist, publicly scolded organizers: "Real men don't put their children on the firing line."

The use of children also caught the attention of the country's most powerful politicians. Robert F. Kennedy, the United States attorney general and brother of the president, was deeply concerned. Even though he supported civil rights, he urged King and others to abandon the plan. "School children participating in street demonstrations is a dangerous business," Kennedy said. "An injured, maimed or dead child is a price none of us can afford to pay."

However, the success of the Crusade's first day inspired King. On May 2, 1963, more than 600 children were peacefully arrested. The jails overflowed, the mood was hopeful, and the police response was calm. *The New York Times* compared the scene to a school picnic. King quickly put aside his early concerns and supported student involvement. He also reassured parents at rallies. He told them, "Don't worry about your children; they are going to

"Real men don't put their children on the firing line."

Young protesters were arrested and held in a makeshift outdoor jail.

be all right. Don't hold them back if they want to go to jail, for they are not only doing a job for themselves, but for all of America and for all of mankind."

Supporters of segregation also found hope in the Children's Crusade—but a different kind of hope. The media and public might be disgusted by the campaign, they thought, and another blow could set back the entire movement. Segregationists carefully crafted their response so they would appear concerned and sympathetic.

"Whatever our sympathies and loyalties have been in the past, whatever they may be in the future, I cannot condone and you cannot condone the use of children to these ends," Birmingham Mayor Albert Boutwell told the *Times*. "I do not need to emphasize the difference between demonstrations by adults and the terrible danger of involving immature teenagers and younger children."

Likewise, Judge Talbot Ellis was outraged over the surge of children in juvenile court. In the first day of the Children's Crusade, 319 children appeared in Ellis' court, one of them a girl just 8 years old. Judge Ellis told the *Times*, "That's what makes my blood boil."

When the attack dogs and fire hoses came out on the campaign's second day, Birmingham's African-American community quickly rallied behind the children. A. G. Gaston, a prominent African-American businessman who'd opposed recruiting students, saw the fire hoses blasting small girls while he talked on the phone. He said, "I can't talk to you now or ever. My people are out there fighting for their lives and my freedom. I have to go help them."

Despite the powerful blasts of water and the use of attack dogs, demonstrators didn't suffer serious injuries. That fact didn't save the reputation of Birmingham's police and firefighters, though. The brutal images in the newspapers and magazines, and on TV, shaped public opinion.

"My people are out there fighting for their lives and my freedom. I have to go help them."

The use of dogs and fire hoses on protesters prompted many public figures to speak out against the Birmingham police department's harsh tactics.

"The photographs of Bull Connor's police dogs lunging at the marchers in Birmingham did as much as anything to transform the national mood," historian Arthur Schlesinger said.

The fact that Carolyn Maull was a girl also influenced Americans' reaction to the city's response. Moore's famous fire hose photo included two teenage boys. But decades later, Carolyn is the person who remains linked to the harsh response. Americans thought differently about women and girls in 1963 than they do today. Women had won the right to vote only 43 years earlier, and the careers they could choose were limited compared with those of men. Many Americans thought girls needed protection.

In the photograph, Carolyn's small body appears powerless against the blast of water, and her dress and earrings emphasize her femininity. As a young girl, she was the campaign's perfect victim. Her mistreatment captured public attention much like the mistreatment of another civil rights icon: Rosa Parks, the Montgomery woman who refused to give up her bus seat to a white passenger.

Charles Moore photographed a young protester knocked down by water from a fire hose.

Public officials could not ignore the growing concern of Americans. U.S. Senator Wayne Morse of Oregon compared Bull Connor and the Birmingham police to the German Nazis, who murdered millions of Jews. Popular entertainers such as folksinger Joan Baez demanded change. Baez, who was performing nearby, even joined the demonstrators that spring.

After days of demonstrations, Birmingham's business leaders finally agreed to a settlement. The downtown shopping district was in disarray, and businesses were suffering financially. People across the country believed Birmingham was a backward and dangerous city. The businesses couldn't afford the negative media attention.

By May 10 representatives of businesses and the campaign had worked out a plan to begin desegregation in Birmingham. The demonstrations ended, and the jailed demonstrators were released. Within two years Congress passed two major civil rights laws. U.S. Senator Jacob Javits of New York credited Moore's photographs with helping to quicken the passage of the Civil Rights Act of 1964, which ended legal racial discrimination in the United States.

"The photographs were never about me," Moore said. "They were always about the people who were laying their lives on the line for basic civil rights. I look back and I can't believe there was ever a time in this country when ANY citizen could not vote. ... I'm very proud of the fact the photographs have been recognized for years. Pictures can and do make a difference. Strong images of historical events do have an impact on society. They can help with change."

"Pictures can and do make a difference."

Chapter Four

THE STRUGGLE CONTINUES

Carolyn Maull's story didn't end with the fire hoses, and the campaign for civil rights in Birmingham didn't end with the desegregation plan. The agreement launched a new chapter in the fight for civil rights. And once again, Carolyn found herself in the center of history.

When details about the agreement spread through the country, many African-Americans thought it fell far short of their goals. They wanted immediate action, but the agreement mostly called for change over time. On the other hand, many white business owners believed the agreement demanded too much, too soon.

Both white and black leaders tried to bring calm back to Birmingham. "We call upon all citizens, white and colored, to continue their calm attitude, to stop rumors and to thank God for a chance to re-establish racial peace," said Sidney Smyer, a white businessman who helped shape the agreement.

But calm was not coming to Birmingham. The Ku Klux Klan expressed rage over the agreement. Klansmen believed police and firefighters should have cracked down harder on the demonstrators. The police handled the kids too gently, they said, and Americans fell victim to "media lies." The Klan accused civil rights leaders of attacking white freedom and ruining Birmingham.

Carolyn, meanwhile, returned to school and church, friends and family. She'd just marched in one of history's

"We call upon all citizens, white and colored, to continue their calm attitude, to stop rumors and to thank God for a chance to re-establish racial peace."

Entertainer Dick Gregory (right, with sign) was arrested during the Children's Crusade and spent four days in jail. He spoke to a large gathering in Birmingham a few weeks later.

most important demonstrations, and her picture would soon capture the world's attention. But her daily life wasn't filled with politics. At age 14, she didn't pay attention to what followed the desegregation agreement.

"I remember visiting a lot of places with my grandparents and parents, but I don't remember any conversations about the racial situation in Birmingham," Maull said years later. "I think they probably whispered among themselves about those kinds of things. The problem was, how can they tell you about it without scaring you? If you grow up in a family with lots of love, sometimes you don't know how bad things are. You don't want to share all the horror stories with children until they get a perspective."

As photos from the demonstration appeared in the world's newspapers and magazines, racial tension in Birmingham reappeared. The Birmingham Board of Education expelled 1,000 students who had marched in the demonstrations. The NAACP appealed and lost. Jim Bevel, the organizer of the Children's Crusade, responded by planning a boycott of schools and businesses. Civil rights leaders feared that the desegregation agreement would collapse under the stress of a boycott. But in the end, a judge sent the kids back to school.

On May 11 the Ku Klux Klan launched its own demonstrations. More than 2,000 people gathered outside Birmingham to protest the desegregation agreement. They burned crosses and passed out fliers urging white citizens to fight back. Police watched the rally but made no arrests.

"If you grow up in a family with lots of love, sometimes you don't know how bad things are."

KU KLUX KLAN

Ku Klux Klan members burned crosses to incite fear in those they tormented.

The Ku Klux Klan formed after the Civil War, when slaves in the United States were freed. The Klan wanted to preserve the "old" South and maintain white power. Klansmen used terror to achieve their goals. They threatened, beat, and killed African-Americans. Whites who supported African-American rights also were targets.

The Klan has had three waves of activity. The first wave covered a period following the Civil War. The second period began in the early 1900s. Klansmen then also targeted Jews and Catholics. They argued that immigrants were destroying the United States, and they feared that communism would take over the country. The Klan's second wave lost steam because of laws banning its tactics. And

the Depression crippled the economy, so members could no longer afford to support the group.

The civil rights movement provoked a third wave of Klan activity in the 1950s and 1960s. Determined to enforce segregation, Klansmen beat and killed civil rights workers. They also bombed their homes. Birmingham suffered so many bombings that it was called "Bombingham."

Despite losing the battle over segregation, the Klan continues to operate today. Klansmen promote "white power" and endorse the use of violence to achieve their goals. Today's Klan also opposes immigration, the desegregation of schools, and affirmative action, a policy that increases racial and gender diversity in schools and jobs.

That night two bombs exploded at the Birmingham home of A. D. King, the brother of Martin Luther King Jr. The family miraculously was not injured.

Then another rumble shook the night. A second bombing hit the Gaston Motel, one of the headquarters of the Birmingham civil rights campaign. Klansmen thought Martin Luther King Jr. would be sleeping in his room, but he hadn't returned from a speech. Although the explosion destroyed part of the motel, there were no injuries.

Shortly after the explosions, African-Americans took to the streets. They came from their homes, from bars,

The Ku Klux Klan detonated a bomb in the Gaston Motel, one of the headquarters of the Birmingham campaign, destroying a part of the building.

from all corners of the city. This group had little interest in the principles of nonviolence. A full-blown riot erupted. Enraged, they threw rocks at police who arrived at the scene. They destroyed phone booths and cars. Someone set fire to a grocery store, and the flames swept through neighboring buildings. Fire trucks and police cars couldn't move through the tightly packed crowd.

The King family and other civil rights leaders clung to their principles of nonviolence. The photos of peaceful demonstrators attacked by police had shifted public opinion in their favor. They couldn't allow their people to riot, no matter what had happened.

A. D. King, whose home had been destroyed just hours earlier, jumped on top of a police car and shouted at rioters through a bullhorn. He begged the crowd to stop the violence, telling them the night's bombings did not justify a violent response. "We're not mad at anyone. We're saying, 'Father, forgive them because they know not what they do.'" Other civil rights leaders climbed into emergency vehicles. They hoped the crowd would allow the fire trucks onto the scene if they saw African-Americans in the front seats.

Police confined reporters to an area by the Gaston Motel, fearing they'd be hurt if they wandered in the crowd. Then police released tear gas.

The crowd scattered by daylight. America's first modern-day race riot devastated a 20-block area. Glass littered the streets, buildings smoldered, and destroyed vehicles blocked intersections. The media reported stories about the riot, but

"Father, forgive them because they know not what they do."

photos and news footage were limited because police tried to block photographers from entering the area.

President Kennedy sent federal troops to bases near Birmingham in case the riots continued. Across the South, African-American children began to copy the children in Birmingham. They marched against segregation, following the nonviolent principles and going to jail without fighting police.

Members of the U.S. Congress began to realize that the country couldn't solve the conflict over civil rights one city at a time. The United States needed a national solution. In a June 1963 speech, President Kennedy said, "Now the time has come for this nation to fulfill its promise. The events in Birmingham and elsewhere have so increased the cries for equality that no city or State or legislative body can prudently choose to ignore them."

Klansmen ignored the president's call for change. They planned another bombing designed to strike at the heart of the civil rights movement: the 16th Street Baptist Church. Civil rights supporters had used the church as a base for campaign activities since early spring.

Carolyn Maull and her family were longtime members of the church. On the morning of September 15, 1963, Carolyn collected attendance reports from Sunday school. As she walked down the stairs, four of her girlfriends gathered in a restroom, where they dressed in choir robes for the morning service.

Suddenly an explosion rocked the building.

"I heard somebody say, 'Hit the floor!'" Carolyn said.

"Now the time has come for this nation to fulfill its promise."

"I just fell on the floor with all the stuff I was holding. The explosion sounded like rumbling thunder. I remember thinking there must be a storm outside. As soon as I thought that, the windows started shattering. Then I heard the sound of many feet. I could hear people getting up, so I did too. We all went out through a back entrance, and once I got outside, I saw a hole in the side of the church where the stairs had been."

The Reverend John Cross stood next to the 16th Street Baptist Church following the bombing by the Ku Klux Klan.

The bomb killed the four girls in the restroom: Denise McNair, Carole Robertson, Addie Mae Collins, and Cynthia Wesley. Two dozen other church members were injured. Three men would eventually be charged with the bombing, two of them not until 40 years later.

Nearly 8,000 people attended the girls' funeral. Martin

Carolyn Maull's four friends, (from left to right) 11-year-old Denise McNair and 14-year-olds Carole Robertson,

Luther King Jr. led the service. "The Holy Scripture says, 'A little child shall lead them,'" he said. "The death of these little children may lead our whole Southland from the low road of man's inhumanity to man to the high road of peace and brotherhood."

Birmingham's children—and all those who sacrificed for

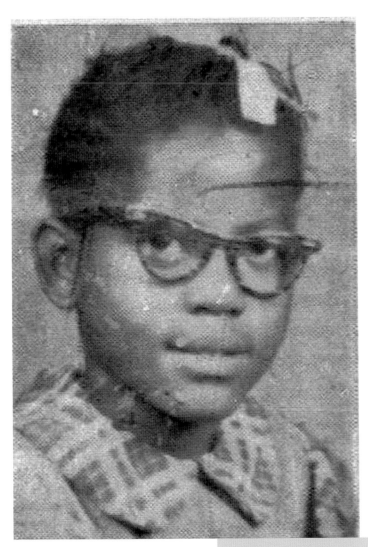

Addie Mae Collins, and Cynthia Wesley, were all killed in the bombing of Birmingham's 16th Street Baptist Church.

civil rights, both black and white—helped lead Americans closer to "peace and brotherhood," as King described it. Within two years Congress passed two major laws. The first, the Civil Rights Act of 1964, outlawed segregation and extended voting rights. The second, the Voting Rights Act of 1965, banned voting practices that for years had kept African-Americans away from the polls.

Charles Moore's powerful photographs of the civil rights movement played an important role in prompting this legislation. Of his work, Moore's photograph of three teens

Charles Moore's photographs helped pave the way for important civil rights legislation.

being slammed against a building has often been singled out. It has been recognized many times for its historic importance. *Life* included it in its collection of the 100 photographs that changed the world, as well as its "Great Pictures of the Century." *American Heritage* magazine included the photograph in its list, "10 Indispensable Photos of the Past 50 Years."

Moore continued to photograph the civil rights movement after the Birmingham campaign. Eventually he became emotionally numb and exhausted from covering the beatings, riots, and killings. He said, "I had been involved in so much ugliness and I realized that I needed to do something else." Moore shifted his career to nature and travel photography. He died in 2010 at the age of 79.

Carolyn Maull McKinstry still lives in Birmingham and attends the 16th Street Baptist Church. She occasionally speaks at conferences and gives interviews about being a child of the civil rights movement. Of Birmingham, she says, "It's become a really nice place to live."

Together she and Charles Moore created one of the most memorable images of the civil rights movement. The Birmingham photographs helped transform the city—and the country—by turning Americans into witnesses at a time when hate and prejudice were on trial. Speeches from leaders such as Martin Luther King Jr. touched the nation's heart, and the image of a terrified young girl tore at its soul.

"It's become a really nice place to live."

Charles Moore's photograph of Carolyn Maull and two unidentified teenage boys helped rally support for civil rights and has become an iconic photo of the struggle for equality.

Timeline

April 3, 1963

Civil rights leaders launch Project C (for Confrontation), a campaign to start desegregating Birmingham, Alabama. Leaders plan for local residents to march and get arrested, overfilling the jails.

Demonstrators begin a series of small sit-ins and meetings. The news reports are short and buried in newspapers' inside pages.

Early April 1963

Late April 1963

An organizer, the Reverend James Bevel, suggests that Project C use children as marchers. Leaders discuss the idea, but they disagree with Bevel.

"A movement is when people actually do out of conviction."

King and Abernathy return to Project C after posting bail. To this point, few adults have been willing to march and risk arrest. The jails are not overflowing.

April 22, 1963

April 10, 1963

City officials get a late-night order from a judge. The order forbids civil rights leaders, including Martin Luther King Jr., from marching and protesting.

April 12, 1963

King and his partner Ralph Abernathy ignore the order and march through Birmingham. Police arrest them.

April 16, 1963

King begins writing his famous "Letter from Birmingham Jail" to explain the need for demonstrations.

April 26, 1963

King and Abernathy return to their homes for the weekend and leave Bevel in charge.

Bevel holds a youth rally and recruits students to march and go to jail.

April 27, 1963

April 29, 1963

Bevel hands out leaflets at schools urging students to skip school and join the demonstration. Other leaders reluctantly agree to the plan, called the Children's Crusade.

Timeline

May 3, 1963

Hundreds of students arrive at the church for the second day of the Children's Crusade. Jails are full, so police use threats and force to contain students. Photographer Charles Moore takes pictures of the firefighters using their hoses on children.

May 2, 1963

Nearly 1,000 children miss school and head to the 16th Street Baptist Church to begin the march. Hundreds are arrested during the protest.

President John F. Kennedy speaks to the nation on television. He calls for laws to ensure that all Americans have civil rights, regardless of skin color.

June 11, 1963

"I saw a hole in the side of the church where the stairs had been."

September 15, 1963

The Klan bombs the 16th Street Baptist Church, a key location for the civil rights movement in Birmingham. Four young African-American girls die.

May 4, 1963

Demonstrations continue. Some white businesspeople want to meet with African-American leaders to discuss their demands and end the demonstrations.

White and African-American leaders reach a settlement. They agree to a plan to begin desegregation.

May 10, 1963

May 11, 1963

In protest, the Ku Klux Klan bombs the home of King's brother and a black-owned motel. A riot breaks out.

"Father, forgive them because they know not what they do."

July 2, 1964

President Lyndon Johnson signs into law the Civil Rights Act of 1964, which outlaws segregation.

August 6, 1965

Johnson signs into law the Voting Rights Act of 1965, which removes barriers that had prevented African-Americans from voting.

Glossary

activists: people who act vigorously to support or oppose one side of a controversial issue

adversary: someone who fights or argues against another

assassinate: to murder someone who is well-known or important, such as a president

civil rights: individual rights that all members of a society have to freedom and equal treatment under the law

discrimination: unfair treatment of a person or group, often because of race, religion, gender, sexual preference, or age

implicates: suggests involvement with

indignities: acts that offend a person's sense of dignity or self-respect

influential: having the power to change or affect someone or something

loitering: being in a public place with no reason; it is illegal in certain places and circumstances

recruit: to try to persuade a person to join

sit-in: form of protest in which one or more people peacefully occupy an area

tactics: plans or methods to win a game or battle or achieve a goal

Additional Resources

Further Reading

Boerst, William J. *Marching in Birmingham*. Greensboro, N.C.: Morgan Reynolds Publishing, 2008.

Corrigan, Jim. *The 1960s Decade in Photos: Love, Freedom, and Flower Power*. Berkeley Heights, N.J.: Enslow Publishers, 2010.

Mayer, Robert H. *When the Children Marched: The Birmingham Civil Rights Movement*. Berkeley Heights, N.J.: Enslow Publishers, 2008.

McWhorter, Diane. *A Dream of Freedom: The Civil Rights Movement From 1954–1968*. New York: Scholastic, 2004.

Internet Sites

Use FactHound to find Internet sites related to this book. All of the sites on FactHound have been researched by our staff.

Here's all you do:
Visit *www.facthound.com*
Type in this code: 9780756543983

Source Notes

Page 7, line 15: Juan Williams. *My Soul Looks Back in Wonder: Voices of the Civil Rights Experience*. New York: Sterling, 2004, p. 78.

Page 10, line 16: "Oral History: Charles Moore." 26 Oct. 2010. http://venetianred.files.wordpress.com/2010/03/charles-moore-interview.pdf

Page 12, line 23: Ibid.

Page 16, sidebar, line 17: Andrew M. Manis. *A Fire You Can't Put Out: The Civil Rights Life of Birmingham's Reverend Fred Shuttlesworth*. Tuscaloosa: University of Alabama Press, 1999, p. 221.

Page 17, lines 7, 12, and 25: John Kaplan. "Charles Moore: The *Life* Magazine Civil Rights Photographs, 1958–1965." Powerful Days: Charles Moore's *Life* Magazine Photographs. 7 Oct. 2010. www.viscom.ohiou.edu/oldsite/moore.site/Pages/AboutMoore.html

Page 23, sidebar, lines 1 and 29: War and World Religions. 26 Oct. 2010. www.ppu.org.uk/learn/infodocs/st_religions.html

Page 25, line 9: Donald L. Grant. *The Way It Was in the South: The Black Experience in Georgia*. Athens: University of Georgia Press, 1993, p. 408.

Page 27, line 24: Glenn T. Eskew. *But for Birmingham: The Local and National Movements in the Civil Rights Struggle*. Chapel Hill: University of North Carolina Press, 1997, p. 250.

Page 28, line 11: Diane McWhorter. *Carry Me Home: Birmingham, Alabama: The Climactic Battle of the Civil Rights Revolution*. New York: Simon & Schuster, 2001, p. 355.

Page 29, line 7: Ibid., p. 364.

Page 31, line 12: "Charles Moore: The *Life* Magazine Civil Rights Photographs, 1958–1965."

Page 33, line 5: William Raspberry. Hodding Carter Lecture on Civil Rights and the Press. 21 April 2005. 26 Oct. 2010. Syracuse University. http://civilrightsandthepress.syr.edu/pdfs/Raspberry%20Lecture%20Transcript.pdf

Page 34, line 13: "Charles Moore: The *Life* Magazine Civil Rights Photographs, 1958–1965."

Page 36, line 11: *A Fire You Can't Put Out: The Civil Rights Life of Birmingham's Reverend Fred Shuttlesworth*, p. 370.

Page 36, lines 18 and 28: "Nation: Dogs, Kids, & Clubs." *Time*. 10 May 1963. 26 Oct. 2010. www.time.com/time/magazine/article/0,9171,830260,00.html

Page 38, lines 4, 14, and 21: Foster Hailey. "Dogs and Hoses Repulse Negroes at Birmingham." *The New York Times*. 4 May 1963. 12 Sept. 2010. http://partners.nytimes.com/library/national/race/050463race-ra.html

Page 39, line 1: Patricia Sullivan. "Charles Moore dies, 79; photographed civil rights violence." *The Washington Post*. 16 March 2010. 26 Oct. 2010. www.washingtonpost.com/wp-dyn/content/article/2010/03/15/AR2010031503450.html

Page 41, line 21: "Charles Moore: The *Life* Magazine Civil Rights Photographs, 1958–1965."

Page 42, line 13: Ibid.

Page 44, line 5: *My Soul Looks Back in Wonder*, p. 77.

Page 47, line 17: *Carry Me Home: Birmingham, Alabama: The Climactic Battle of the Civil Rights Revolution*, p. 422.

Page 48, line 11: John F. Kennedy. "Radio and Television Report to the American People on Civil Rights." 11 June 1963. 10 Oct. 2010. John F. Kennedy Presidential Library and Museum. www.jfklibrary.org/Historical+Resources/Archives/Reference+Desk/Speeches/JFK/003POF03CivilRights06111963.htm

Page 48, line 28: *My Soul Looks Back in Wonder*, p. 75.

Page 51, line 1: Martin Luther King Jr. "Eulogy for the Martyred Children." 18 Sept. 1963. MLKOnline. 26 Oct. 2010. www.mlkonline.net/eulogy.html

Page 54, lines 11 and 19: "Charles Moore: The *Life* Magazine Civil Rights Photographs, 1958–1965."

Select Bibliography

Durham, Michael. *Powerful Days: The Civil Rights Photography of Charles Moore*. New York: Stewart, Tabouri and Chang, 1991.

Eskew, Glen T. *But for Birmingham: The Local and National Movements in the Civil Rights Struggle*. Chapel Hill: University of North Carolina Press, 1997.

"Eyes on the Prize: America's Civil Rights Movement." 1954–1985. American Experience. PBS. 10 Oct. 2010. www.pbs.org/wgbh/amex/eyesontheprize/

Grant, Donald L. *The Way It Was in the South: The Black Experience in Georgia*. Athens: University of Georgia Press, 1993.

Hailey, Foster. "Dogs and Hoses Repulse Negroes at Birmingham." *The New York Times*. 4 May 1963. 12 Sept. 2010. http://partners.nytimes.com/library/national/race/050463race-ra.html

Kaplan, John. "Charles Moore: The *Life* Magazine Civil Rights Photographs, 1958–1965." Powerful Days: Charles Moore's *Life* Magazine Photographs." 7 Oct. 2010. www.viscom.ohiou.edu/oldsite/moore.site/Pages/AboutMoore.html

Kennedy, John F. "Radio and Television Report to the American People on Civil Rights." 11 June 1963. 10 Oct. 2010. John F. Kennedy Presidential Library and Museum. www.jfklibrary.org/Historical+Resources/Archives/Reference+Desk/Speeches/JFK/003POF03CivilRights06111963.htm

Manis, Andrew M. *A Fire You Can't Put Out: The Civil Rights Life of Birmingham's Reverend Fred Shuttlesworth*. Tuscaloosa: University of Alabama Press, 1999.

McWhorter, Diane. *Carry Me Home: Birmingham, Alabama: The Climactic Battle of the Civil Rights Revolution*. New York: Simon & Schuster, 2001.

Raspberry, William. Hodding Carter Lecture on Civil Rights and the Press. 21 April 2005. 26 Oct. 2010. Syracuse University. http://civilrightsandthepress.syr.edu/pdfs/Raspberry%20Lecture%20Transcript.pdf

Sullivan, Patricia. "Charles Moore dies, 79; photographed civil rights violence." *The Washington Post*. 16 March 2010. 26 Oct. 2010. www.washingtonpost.com/wp-dyn/content/article/2010/03/15/AR2010031503450.html

"They Fight a Fire That Won't Go Out." *Life*. 17 May 1963, pp. 27–36.

Transcript. "Setting the Scene: The Landscape of Civil Rights and Press Coverage." Civil Rights and the Press Symposium. 24 April 2004. S.I. Newhouse School of Public Communications, Syracuse University, New York.

Transcript. "MLK Papers: Words That Changed a Nation." CNN. 7 Feb. 2010. 12 Sept. 2010. http://transcripts.cnn.com/TRANSCRIPTS/1002/07/siu.01.html

Williams, Juan. *My Soul Looks Back in Wonder: Voices of the Civil Rights Experience*. New York: Sterling, 2004.

Index